Lost and Somewhere Else

Lost and Somewhere Else

Jenny Bornholdt

Victoria University Press

VICTORIA UNIVERSITY PRESS
Victoria University of Wellington
PO Box 600 Wellington
vup.victoria.ac.nz

Copyright © Jenny Bornholdt 2019
First published 2019

Illustrations by Elizabeth Thomson, reproduced with
kind permission of the artist. Both images first appeared in
Elizabeth Thomson – Cellular Memory, edited by Gregory
O'Brien, Aratoi – Wairarapa Museum of Art and History, 2018
p. 34: detail from *Freedom and Structure – light and waves*, 2017
pp.38–39: detail from *Tatio*, 2014–2017

ISBN 9781776562862

A catalogue record is available from the National Library
of New Zealand

Printed in China by 1010 Printing Group International

to Greg

Contents

Lost and Somewhere Else

Lost and Somewhere Else

Where do I stand?
Usually
in the little square of sunlight
by the back door.
From there I can see
our bridesmaid rhododendron,
beans and peas
level pegging it
in the garden
and the washing –
last few days' worth
on the line. The shirt
he wore to talk about
paintings, Monday's
T-shirt, shorts
from lost
and found, dress
my grandmother would've
disapproved of:

Put something else on
you look like a
fun day animal.

Typhoon

Slug tracery on the shed.
Birds carry on
over bread
in the tree
young thrushes' breasts
shimmer in the sun,
their throats atremble
with song.

The light on the tree
and the fence
is so suggestive of the past
that I go there. To my sisters
under one roof.
To my mother and father
there also,
my grandmother's
two-bar Typhoon
heating the room.

Storm

A day so full of promise
you might kiss
your own arm.
The baby bowls
our gathered avocados
across the kitchen floor's
worn lino. We
bowl them back, then
step outside to where
there's always air
to go around. We breathe
our share, watch
as a mountain range of clouds,
edges lit like art,
moves in.
This morning someone mowed
an oval in the grass
around the cottage.
Outside the mown border all is wild,
roaring. Inside, the grass is groomed,
serene, just like the lawn the year
our childhoods upped a gear.
Elm trees elderly, autumnal.
Beneath them
our father and an uncle locked
in combat, fringed
by the herbaceous border.

Becoming Girl

Becoming girl. What *was*
that? The girl and
the becoming? Hair
like venetian blinds, all
the lesser excellencies
turned to stone. The stone quarried
to become road – Eddy Ave
which leads to Carillon
where mothers count their way
to sanity – down which the bus travels
to where you need and most want
to go. To where you and your friend,
who you've known since you began
to remember, become zebras
as the light falls down the sky;
to where all your best answers
are afterwards. All the while becoming
girl, lost, and tender as steak
or as the tree on an island
named for a Portuguese exclamation,
the tree whose trunk you stroke
and all its branches quiver.

Finance

City bracketed by snow
woollens airborne
in the hall.
Starved, our animal selves
tore grass
from the lawn, bark
from the trees, trotted
to where our children
gnawed the bones of animals
smaller than themselves.

Was this the end
of the world? Of childhood?
This frozenness trapping us
in our adult selves.

Who knew what would
happen next. The film festival,
perhaps? A short about
my father's handkerchiefs
making their way
in the world. One gone
to a weeping air hostess,
another to the brow of a young man
knocked from his bike. Who knew
where this would lead us.

By evening
we were done,
though the children still ravenous
for food and experience.
Snow lay like a man's handkerchief
over the hand of a magician.
We expected the coin,
the rabbit, the dove, but nothing . . .
only more snow
and the dollar rising and falling
under cover of darkness.

Careers

Funny night breathing.
All his 'p' words escape
and float to the ceiling

pulmonary
particular
puffball
pandemonium

They fall as rain
on the roof of the house
you dream about – the one
made up of all the houses
you ever lived in –
the one your father visits
to tell you
he is no longer dead.
As he stands at the door
you notice that the path
and the driveway and the front lawn
are beginning to slide down
the hillside you didn't know
you lived on.

The sky pours water
on your head. You wish
you were an engineer
and knew about drainage,
slippage, bracing.
You never would have bought

this dangerous house.
Instead, you know nothing,
except how to think things
and sometimes write them down.

Last Summer

Waihi Beach, January 2016

No hare,
no quail this year.
We're tracking
absence. First
a much-loved aunt
then a potter who,
knowing earth,
asked for burial
worm-deep.
A giant moon
drags the ocean in so high
they close the beach.
We lie at the centre
of night. Darkness
eyes us up.

Dark

It was dark
under the earth.
Death-dark.
Who knew?

The dead, of course,
but knowledge
was beyond them.

Worms
and other creatures
tunnelled
in the gloom.

Tree roots
inched their way about
found anchor
in the dark universe.

None of this
we knew,
being blithe
with light –

waiting for the sun
to rise, then
the moon, bonny
in its sky of night.

Wellington Summer Haiku

It is eight degrees
and the Thorndon outdoor pool
is swimming with leaves.

Anyone but Brahms

Galling to be the one who's named,
but out.

Like being a pool
closed in summer.

Like being told *I've met
someone.* As though
you're not.

Science

What can happen
in a mouse
or a dish?
My heart, that could
happen there. My heart
full of leafy greens.
My heart, which
sometimes, drowning
in circumstance, has to
give a little. Like the apple tree
from Mark and Lucy,
weighed down
by its crop, propped
by Chris's bee frame.

Now autumn's come,
clear and bold
as a Sydney waitress.
Easter and our son
has to write an essay
on 'God's Saving Love'
*I don't even know
what that means*, he says.
I'll google it.

Our new front lawn
fills our hearts
with gladness.
We go outside
and gaze at it. Just gaze

at it, then move deep
into the cooling days,
unpick the cross stitch
of the garden,
clear around the lemon,
the lesser plum.

Woman on a Train, Reading

for Robyn Marsack – on the occasion of
her farewell from the Scottish Poetry Library

She's inside the animal
of the poem – dark,
pungent, locomotive,
driving and driven
by line and break and those
persuasive voices.
There's someone there
from Orkney, a Paris
plum, and landscape hurtling by
in every tone and tongue.
On she reads, through all
the musics, till the train
draws near, draws in,
the din subsides, and she
steps out, arrived.

Hearken

Hearken. This is the blue shirt
that I wear every year. Hearken,
I have been made an orphan
by death, by war, by the water,
by wood. That is all
I have to say. It is ended.
Hearken, this is my word.
My speech ends here. Hearken,
the hairs of my head
have become grey. That is all
I have to say. Hearken, the light
is great. Enough. I have finished.
Hearken little flock, that is all
I have to say. I have finished.
Little orphan, the widow and the poor
I approve of goodness alone, and not
of the many things of the world.
This ends mine. This is mine.
The proverb says: *Leaving the things*
which are behind, I press forward
to those which are before. That is all
I have to say. Enough.

Funeral

The excellent friend
has gone.

I have a plan.
Meet me in town.
Bring the money.

The excellent friend
has gone. He
and his beautiful life
bound for some other music
via organ smudge
and song.

Winter

Cold around my ankles
like a cat.
Light comes off leaves,
red, curled on branches
budded, brokering spring.

We're so seasonal
it hurts.
White camellias stark
against dark green.
The tree's last lemon
a lightbulb
in the dank corner.

Wintersweet

Let me be yours,
the cold so froze
it sets our limbs –
with solace found
by moving
to the heart of it.

Let me be yours,
the season and
the sweet
the flower's scent
intense, a creature's paw
unfurling through the ice
of morning.

Let me be yours,
the cloudy breath of winter
stopped on stately limbs.

Let me be your both –
your winter thaw
your dormouse claw.

Flight

It came to pass
that I boarded a plane
and as I edged past the man
in the aisle seat he said
my name is Dov. I knew
you would come.

So Dov came to pass
and then the next thing
came to pass which was
the plane, which fell through the air
so that all felt and understood
the word 'slew'.

We held the hands of those
next to us. Dov's hand. Dov
who knew I would come.
The hand of my son, who said
hang on, I'll just finish listening
to this song.

And it came to pass
that in those seconds of fall
we entered the deluge zone
which was dark and dangerous
and it came to pass
that we thought things
we hadn't thought before
and understood things
that couldn't be said out

loud or even in our quiet
pulpy insides.

We understood
that children sucked life
from their mothers
then led it back in
in mysterious ways.

We understood
that men damaged children
in shocking unspeakable
ways and in quiet
secretive ways and in silence
and murk.

Somehow
dandelions marjoram
thistle and thrush
came to pass.
And a bank teller
named 'Snow'

And then it came to pass
that we turned away
from where we were headed
because the wind there
was too strong
to land safely on one engine.
We turned away
from the wind bothering the trees,
flaying pansies, knocking lemons
one against another;

away from hymns ancient and
modern; from the holes
dug in the garden for kitchen scraps
which resemble graves
prepared for a succession
of small animals.

Away we turned, back
to a runway on which waited
emergency vehicles
and so it came to pass
that we touched ground
whole, feeling lucky
and afraid.

Being out of danger
it came to pass
that we broke the chain of hands
that held us, though not the chain
of thoughts – that held.
And held. And led us
to the tightly fenced park
where bodies lie, decomposing,
terrifying yet natural,
faces slurred into earth,
and to the deer who come
and delicately nuzzle bone.

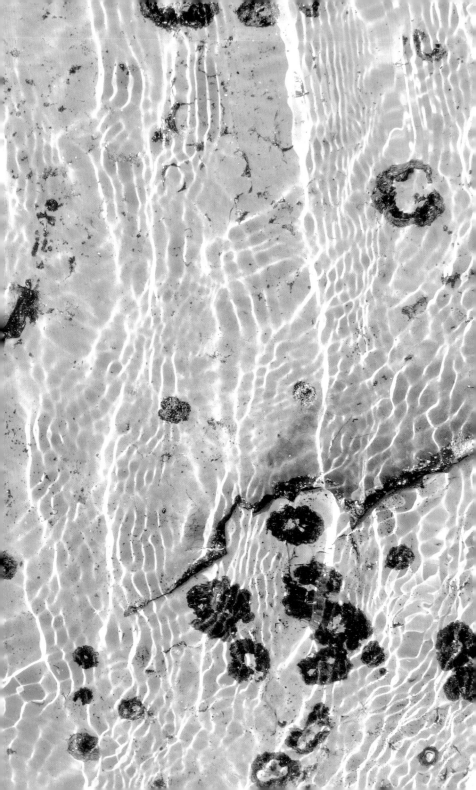

Cellular

for Liz Thomson

Liz, I've been thinking about your works
for months now as I've walked around,
gardened, slept, not slept, trying to find
a way in to all that they are
and this morning, early, when I went up
to my shed, on the grass – what's
left of it after long, dry days – still damp
from dew, was a piece of torn cardboard
like a moth's wing
and when I went behind the shed
to pick roses – Wedding Day – a bee
landed on a held stem and its vibration
travelled through me like a current,
which is close to how I feel when I see
your work. A kind of ignition happens,
along with great quiet. It's like being in water
more particularly the sea when it's cold
and your body tenses then enters and calms.

I'm trying to make sense of this by writing.
I spent yesterday at a poetry conference subtitled
form & fragmentation and the main thing I thought
about
was a silk shirt patterned in deep reds and blues
worn by a tattooed woman whose arms matched
the fabric. She could have been one of your
Inner Raoul works. As the day went by
all the young women at the conference put their hair
up and down, down and up, so I wasn't sure

who was who anymore. Their hair hung long
down their backs, like seaweed or water
or sand trailed through like your *Mahia Beach* works,
then they whorled it up like cockle shells
or Saturn's rings. I came adrift and my brain
so long unmoored
felt formless and open.

When my cousin slept in the gallery while you
hung your show, he lay on a black quilted bench
which could have been one of your moulds.
He looked like an art installation – still and formal –
long concise body neat on the oblong.
His patched-up face and newly-constructed nose
could have done with some beading to shift the focus,
make him whole again.
In the way our plumber, Ian, will hopefully make
our plumbing whole. He's been looking at our drains –
the earth below washed and loosed by water –
the whole shebang a network of memory,
pipes going nowhere. We need to dig, rejoin,
redirect flow; the same with our old crumbling
concrete paths and our wall, cellular. We live in the midst
of your work, our lawn tawny – like sand seen
from way above.

This is my first letter poem and it feels
private and public, closed and not,
like your work. The way you come in close
then pull right back so one thing can be
another; until all seems other

so a cell can be a lizard's skin or seed
or a ball of slime that is a thinking thing
which grows a stem with a pod which explodes
and begins all over again. Remarkable, like
us. Like the way art works. Or poetry.
Like the way a stretch of sand can summon
a dress my mother wore on a date
with my father – him in a dark suit, her
in cream satin, with pearls.

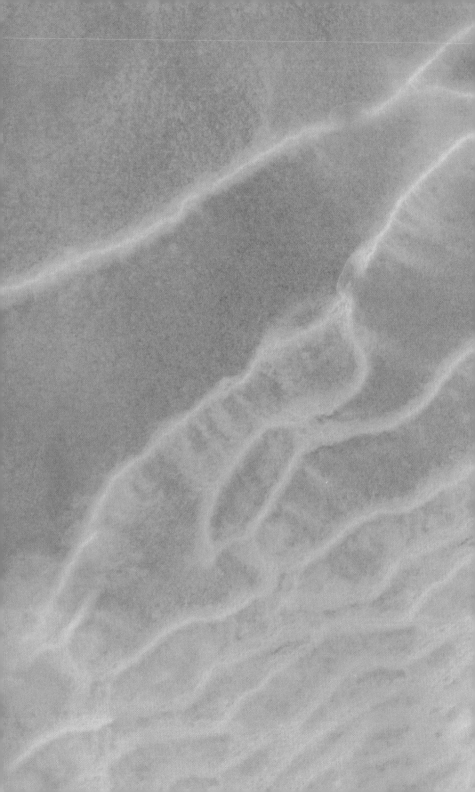

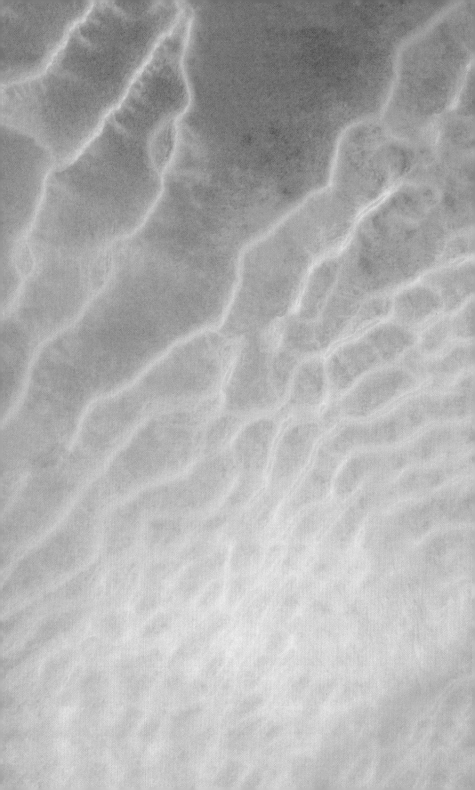

Duck Three Ways

Let's put our mother's
favourite cat socks on
and move to Canada.

*

Let's eat duck
three ways. The first
the way my flatmate hit one
in his car. After bundling the body
into the boot, he
drove home, traumatised,
to tell us. Opened
the boot
and out it flew.

*

Then the way we left one
in a basket on the side of the road
at a French market, with le pain,
la salade . . . *oh merde*

*

The third I've forgotten
unless it was the one the wolf girl
gobbled up, along with all the words
for loss.

*

Let's go to pieces.
Let's not.

*

Let's stop shouting
at the stupid intersection.

*

Let's not worry
about not having a barbecue
since you set the green wheelie bin
on fire with hot ashes
and our new neighbour
had to put the flames out
with his hose.
You vowed to never again
barbecue anything
and that's okay because
if we leave the back door open
our stove is almost outdoors.

*

Let's go to the big leaves
of Auckland, to the lemon trees
in the gardens of the houses
people like us
can't afford to live in
anymore.

*

Let's thank
the lemon trees for their
verdancy.

*

Let's ring our chemical sisters.
Let's go outside
and bark at the over-the-road dog.

*

Let's pick up more
of Parrot Dog's *Four
Dead Canaries*
and carry them
through Moon Gate
to your father
who is 92
and thirsty.

Once-tiny Boys

Once-tiny boys
are balding
I pass them
in the street.
Call them back –
armpit fart, Chinese
burn, blow
to the shin, hard
as you can make it.

Bench

Some days, life resembles
the kitchen bench,
endless as a desert
before you.

Like the one in Australia
a group of elderly people
plan to cross
on motor scooters,
or so your sister tells you –
the one who comes for coffee
so you make another pot,
put water out for her dog,
ask her to please pass the squirrel.

At her school meeting,
when the teacher asked who had read
the newsletter, all the women
put up their hands. A man said
that's mummy's work.

I'd rather be dead
than married to you
my sister said.

Talking with Adrian

At the hydrotherapy pool
Adrian asks everyone what they're having
for dinner.

> *I don't know.*
> *I haven't thought about it yet.*

Will there be pudding?

> *Maybe.*

Will Greg make the dinner? Or your boys?

> *Maybe. That would be good.*
> *Who makes your dinner, Adrian?*

The house makes it.
What are you doing after swimming?

> *I'm going home to lie down.*
> *And read.*
> *What are you doing after swimming?*

Exciting things.

Cultural Studies

England in the 1920s

Cecily's stockings
and strappy shoes
knee-length skirt, top
with round collar
tight-fitting cloche hat.

Croquet was a popular game.
These mallets are for hitting the balls
through the hoops.

Percy's socks and suspenders
two-tone shoes
shirt and tie, tweed
trousers, knitted tanktop
and tweed jacket.
Percy's wool cap.

Tea set in the 'Art Deco' style.

*

America in the 1950s

Ronald's blue jeans
checked shirt
American college football jacket
leather loafer shoes.

Donna's blouse.
Full skirt, cardigan,
wide belt, straw bag.

Nancy's dress and cardigan.
Ankle socks, lace-up
sneakers. Nancy's bag.

Signs for the diner wall.

*

Ancient China

Emperor Yang's embroidered robe.
Outer robe with wide sleeves.

Empress Ji's dress.
Silk robe and embroidered
scarf. Hair with
golden ornaments.

Shengtong's dress,
hair and jacket.

It was the fashion to wear shoes
with long flat toes.

*

Bride and groom (Japan)

Kumiko's geta (sandals)
and tabi (socks).
Silk kimono, obi (belt).
Outer kimono.
Kumiko's hair with lucky
hair pins, cherry blossom hair pin.
Silk purse.

Stick these magnolia flowers
onto the trees.

Toru's kimono, geta (sandals)
and tabi (socks). Obi (belt).
Hakama (pleated skirt)
haori (jacket).

*

Reindeer Herders (Norway)

Put trousers on the reindeer herders
from Norway.
Kofte dresses for Inga and Tilda.
A kofte top for Morten.
Stick these belts on top of the dresses
and Morten's belt on his top.
Put these shawls on Inga and Tilda's
shoulders. Hats and fur boots for
Inga and Tilda. Fur gloves and leather boots
for Morten and a cap
of the four winds.

*

Put Cecily's stockings and strappy shoes
on Percy. A cherry blossom pin
in his hair.
In his kimono beside the magnolia tree
Toru will say 'I do'.

*

Ronald's blue jeans
fit Donna. They look good
with her blouse.
Give her Percy's two-tone
shoes and tweed jacket.
Give her a mallet
so she can whack the croquet balls hard
through the hoops.

*

Nancy's dress and sneakers are okay
but Cecily is stuck in that stupid skirt.
Try her in Emperor Yang's embroidered
robe. It's a perfect fit!
Stick Percy's tweed trousers and knitted tanktop
on Empress Ji. Shentong can have
Donna's full skirt with Ronald's
football jacket.

*

Put Ronald and Emperor Yang
in the diner under the signs.

*

But what about Kumiko?
She's waiting with her lucky hair pins
for Toru, who has just married Percy.
Move her to pages 5&6 where Inga, Tilda
and Morten are herding reindeer.
Inga has a spare kofte dress.
Stick it on Kumiko with Donna's
wide belt.

*

The reindeer are restless.
The wind rises,
carries the scent of moss.
Move Cecily, Donna, Nancy,
Empress Ji and Shentong to pages 5&6.
Shift Inga, Tilda and Morten so there's
room on the sled for their new friends.
Give the command *Hike*
so the reindeer herders' dogs
move off across the snow
towards the four winds.

Cold

It's freezing
out there – minus
one. Pies stacked
in the warmer.
Toaster cord bound
in red tape
like a chilli.

Crossing

Driving across town
she feels plain
and botanical.

At a crossing
there's a man
with a cake, girl
with a tune.
Four young people
wheel a bed,
headed for a house
where a young woman
might read, love a man/some
men, might hold their bodies
close and welcome some parts
of those bodies
into hers.

Years later
she might see these men
in suits and on television and
many years later
might pass one, a house painter,
as she drives to buy
paint, for heaven's sake.

Now, nearing sixty,
this woman loves her husband
ferociously.
When she turns the compost

and finds the flat wrinkled body
of a mouse,
she remembers the time
he rang her in Scotland
to say he'd seen one in the pile
and what should he do?

She shovels the remains
of the mouse with the rest
of the compost to beneath
the blossom, which bows
low and graceful over neglect,
which abounds, as it does,
thankfully, in the garden of the
southern house they move to
for a time.

He's up to his ears
in sadness, both of them aghast
at landscape. Being asthmatic
he is immediately attractive
to animals – at the lake
a fox terrier pup takes shelter
under his chest as he lies down
on a towel after a swim.
In the kitchen a mouse
bumps into his foot. Drama
in the house! Not for the first
time. These were rooms
of costume, scenery,
leading ladies and men
on the front terrace, leaning
on architect Ernst Plischke's rail,

stone warm underfoot, snowed
mountains as backdrop
while the deep, broad river passed
below them, always
on its way.

Almost Haiku

Boys turn into men
go out late and forget
to come home again.

En Plein Air

Horse floats
on the other side
of the river.

Doors open.
Horses
hoove backwards
into the crispy morn.

Fog

Winter, Alexandra, 2018

The moment will come.
Or the month.
Here's July, waiting
around the corner.
Fog disappears the clock,
mountains, town and
the river – which is like
thought – molten, lit,
slipping by.

Geology

Each in our own
deep time, my friend
and I – under trees, beside
water – in the gardens
we were born to.

*

A walnut tree
shaded, housed,
then shed me –
greenstick fracture
of the wrist.

*

Her mother's
rhododendron
on the move.

*

Life's sediment.
Double-dug potato bed.
Tenacious agapanthus.

*

She's planted blossom,
dismantled the herbaceous
border.

*

Crab apples, Japonica,
Sedum, Rose

*

We walk.
Trees elbow over us
for the light.

Blossom

i.m. Marion Antonievich

Your body still
as concentration.
Mind an accordion.

Spring rises. You
out there
in your gardening shoes
trowel in hand
loving every petal
every leaf.

The house fills
with wayward blossom

your children –
grown now –
move through the room
like ballet.

Gone

Your brain
like a walnut, snug
inside its promising shell.

But all's aged now.
Going, gone.
All anger and wrangle
gone.

Family detonates
inside you. Who am I
in my *floral get-up*?
Your brother is coming.
Your sister. Mother. Father.
Wait for them. The train.
The bus. The house. The room.
The book. The man. That man.
The man etherised
upon the table. Who *was* that?

Your son holds your hand
as you listen to Vivaldi
while leaves drift
across a screen.
I put on my floral get-up
and go on out.

It Has Been a Long Time
Since I Last Spoke to You,
So Here I Am

All day
cloud has hovered in a vee of hills
just below the snow-covered
Pisa range. It's nature's joke –
snow / cloud / cloud / snow?
Unfeeling nature, to which we bring
our joys and sads.   Wanting . . .
as if staring at a mountain or a lake
will ease loss.

It has been a long time since I last
spoke to you. Since then
his mother has died
and my uncle. Each Christmas
this kind, gentle man would build
a centrepiece for the table – one year
the Eiffel tower, the menu
French. Next, for Italy,
the Colosseum. Our middle age
is one long goodbye. Even nature
is in danger.

Like in summer
when the hawk struck the sparrow
from beside us on the riverbank.
We were talking, still damp
from swimming, heads

turned to each other so we saw
nothing, just heard the wings' rush,
the smaller bird sound its brief alarm . . .

It has been a long time
since I last spoke to you.
When we were children, our fathers
wanted to be mountains
our mothers were the sky.
So here I am, the dry hands,
steady in fog, waiting by the not-there
trees, the holes birds make
in air.

About

Trees lose their content
to the river.
Down it comes to us
story borne by currents
all the weird logics
loose upon the water.

What Comes

The river brings us
wind, which causes trees
to be percussive.
It sometimes
brings us song.
Once it brought
the sound of divers
as they searched for the boy
who was gone.

Old Prayer

Hawk, as you
lift and flare
above the river's
slide, take us not
in thy talons. Take us not
from the bank
or branch or wrench us
from the earth, lifted by
calamitous wings.
Fix us not with your eye.
Take us not up
the way you raise the sparrow
and the finch. Leave us
as the covey of quail
in the willow.
Leave us be.

Airborne at Mandeville

I hear him
follow the hills
the river's swerve
to the sea.
If the last I know of him
is sound, what
will I do, how
will I be?

Black Shag

She ran towards us,
Julia, though we did not know
her name at the time.
She ran towards us, legs
long, thin and shaky,
knees wild, arms outstretched,
waving. *I'm running*
she called. *I'm running.*

We were outside
the Black Shag café
in Invercargill, just flown in
from Stewart Island.
We shared the plane
with the Island's ambulance driver
and his deaf dog, Kiki,
who travelled on his knee.

The pilot of the plane
was a young man whose
head, when he turned
to face the runway,
was scarred in a half-moon
which rose from one side
of the base of his skull
to the other.

As we came in to land,
the plane in front
turned, then straightened

in line with the runway.
We, too, turned, but our arc
was tighter and we appeared
to be headed for a field.

I looked at the pilot's head
with its scar, looked again
at the ground, then saw
a mown strip.
After landing, the young man
laughed, said *we decide ahead.*
I asked for the grass.

*

I'm running because I can,
because it feels so good.
I couldn't and now I can.
I'm on a new drug – I have MS –
and it means I can run,
so I do, all the time.
I was diagnosed at 20,
over the phone. They said
'you have MS', like, 'you have
a cold'. I didn't even know
what it was. And now
I'm running. My name
is Julia. The coffee here
is great and I'm running
to get some.

Spring, Alexandra

August, September,
come down off the wall.
October fills the air
with poplar fluff, like snow,
but rising. Like asparagus
in the garden – rogue crop
seeded from an orderly bed.
Spears hidden in grass, beside
tea-coloured iris, a clump
in the glasshouse skeleton, grass
thigh-high, the river below
running like story
where everything matters
but all passes.

Later, we hear children yell
as they swing out and let go
over the water. Again
and again they do this
until the light and we
are gone.

Something is Everywhere

i.m. Jack O'Brien

Asparagus everywhere
in the garden, like eggs
laid by wayward hens.
The river, too, is
everywhere, rising up
over the stone wall, over
grass and the track,
the boardwalk now
an underwater path
through trees, which
still send fluff everywhere –
into our rooms, our hair.
Dogs are everywhere.
They bring their something
fur on their something bodies
and sniff and run around
while their owners look
at the everywhere river and think
of somewhere, elsewhere.
Everywhere inside a book
was the place my father-in-law
longed to go. Books being
like the river – something
and everywhere – beauty pooled
in their lines of type.

Ice Likely

An hour is quail
on the lawn, heaven
to a companionable
horse. The smell of hedgehog
to a blind dog.
Fire ticking
in its box.

An hour is how
music feels.

An hour is the river.
Poplar fluff enough
for a pillow
for a dying woman –
not dying yet, not now,
but soon.

It's a rock-strewn paddock.
A fence of time
within which stands
an aunt on the road
in her nightdress
bewildered and cold.

It's a road sign
Ice Likely

It's all that we need
all that it takes.

Notes and Acknowledgements

Some of these poems have previously been published in *Sport*, *Best New Zealand Poems*, *Poetry* (US) and *Cyphers* (Ireland).

'Lost and Somewhere Else' was handprinted and illustrated by Brendan O'Brien in 2016 in a limited edition of 9.

'Anyone but Brahms' comes from Catalan composer Federico Mompou, who, when asked to name his favourite composer, said, 'Everyone except Brahms.'

'Hearken' is a found poem, with text taken from *Maori Messenger: Te Karere Maori*, Vol 1, Issue 12, 2 September 1861.

'Wintersweet' was written for and published in *Black Barn – Portrait of a Place*, written by Jenny Bornholdt and Gregory O'Brien (Penguin, 2018).

'Cellular' was written in response to the work of Liz Thomson and published in the monograph *Elizabeth Thomson – Cellular Memory* (Aratoi, 2018).

'Cultural Studies' is a found poem using text from children's sticker books, with interference from the author.

Thanks to Franka Moleta for the title of the poem 'It Has Been a Long Time Since I Last Spoke to You, So Here I Am'.

Grateful thanks to the members of the Henderson Trust, who invited me and Gregory O'Brien to have the unforgettable experience of living in the Ernst Plischke–designed Henderson House, Alexandra, Central Otago, from January 2018 to January 2019. Thanks especially to Grahame and Fiona Sydney for their friendship and generosity during this time.